The Power of Choice
Raising Children Who Choose Well

The Power of Choice *Raising Children Who Choose Well*

Copyright © 2018 by Lydia O'Leary. All Rights Reserved.

Cover Design by Kathleen Clark
Cover Photo by Heather Wilson
Author Photo by Kathy Poumakis

Scriptures taken from the Holy Bible, New International Version.
ISBN 978-0692962350

Printed in the United States of America

*This book is dedicated to God, first
and foremost, for without You and Your
incredible love, we would all be lost.
YOU are our hope.
To Jim, my partner in life, by best friend and
husband. There is no one I would rather
figure out this journey with than you.
It is also dedicated to our wonderful,
crazy, full of life, laughter-loving kiddo's.
You guys are the most loving, welcoming,
accepting truth seekers I know.
Always stay awesome!*

Table of Contents

Preface 1

1. Establishing the Goals................................. 6

2. Being a Parent on Purpose 12

3. Teaching the "Why Factor" 18

4. Establish Choice and Consequence s........... 26

5. Teaching Personal Responsibility 40

6. Honestly Speaking 51

7. Pointing Your Child to Jesus 61

8. Letting Them Grow and
   Letting Them Go 75

PREFACE
Love and Choice

[1]The breath of God hovered and swirled as tendrils of life-giving words brought forth a world so immensely different from what we now know. The heavens, the vast expanse where stars and galaxies lay far beyond even the grandest of imaginations of the time, exploded into an unending race to forever.

The sunlight glistened through the lush green vegetation, as they rapidly emerged their heads above the ground for the first time, while animals tenderly tried out their God given forms as they stretched and frolicked and played.

And then, the crowning moment of creation, when up from the dust, and one joined into another, humankind was born. The offspring of God Himself, those made in His very image, bearing His likeness. The beauty of God in human form, made from the very dust He had created. And God looked and saw that ALL that He had created was good.

And there we pause. If only the story could have stopped there. How many times have we read

---

1 Genesis 1-3

this passage and wondered "Why? Why would God *ruin* it all by giving them a choice?" It could have stayed perfect. It WOULD have stayed perfect. Why would God create a tree such as this; one that gave the knowledge of good and evil but was strictly off limits? If it was so wrong, why even create it?

How does something like this fit in to the perfection of the garden. This tree of "choice" was deemed "good" with the rest of creation but at the same time man was not supposed to eat from it. What was its purpose?

This is one of those moments in Scripture when God reveals something so deeply strong about Himself (Love).

If you have ever experienced the heartache of fully entrusting yourself to another person only to have them utterly reject you, you can understand the strength I am talking about. The kind of strength that in that moment of heartache does not build a wall, but instead chooses to again give freely.

God was not unaware of the devastation that would come with giving mankind this choice. Scripture says that before the foundations of the world were laid, Christ was crucified. God knew that choice would open the door to allow for inevitable heartache. Yet He still did it. Why?

What did God see beyond the possibility of pain? It must have been something greater. It must have been something more powerful or immense to make it worth it.

What other choice was God putting before Adam and Eve? He was giving them the possibility to obey Him, to trust Him, to trust His love for them and, in doing so, to love Him back. In fact right next to this tree of "choice" was another tree, a tree that showed the other option; The Tree of Life.

God had placed such a better choice in front of them. What would they have experienced had they chosen differently?

God knew that LOVE RETURNED was worth it. That it wasn't even comparable to the heartache of broken relationship. The same can be said for our lives.

There MUST be something SO MUCH MORE POWERFUL about the choice to love back.

It is easy to point the finger at our earliest of ancestors, declaring their foolishness. But one must take a sober assessment of ourselves before we can cast any blame. Have we ever looked to our own understanding, choosing our own way over the way that God says is best? Of course, we have. But as much as one choice has passed us, another is always before us. What will we choose today? For the mercy of God is new every morning.

In Deuteronomy 30 God, again, lays out a choice to His people,

19 "I call heaven and earth to witness against you today, that I have set before you life and death, the blessing and the curse. So, choose life in order that you may live, you and your descendants,"

God does not present each choice independent of what will follow. With each choice comes a consequence. While choosing life will bring a blessing, choosing death will bring a curse.

And then we see it again; as God places Himself into the throes of humanity, to come and purchase our freedom through His death and resurrection, God presents humanity with a choice.[2] And He calls us to choose wisely- to count the cost of following Him so we are not taken unaware by the results of our decision.

I recently heard Ravi Zacharias speak to an audience regarding choice and consequence. And what he said describes so perfectly the way God has designed choice for us.

---

[2] Luke 14:25-34

"Consequences are bound to the choices you make. You can have your choice, but you cannot choose your consequence." ~Ravi

So where does this leave us? There are so many directions that we can take this but for the purposes of this book we will stick to the topic at hand, *"Teaching our children to choose well."*

CHAPTER ONE
Establishing the Goal

My husband Jim and I have now brought 4 children into this world, each one so incredibly special, and so incredibly different, from the others.

Yet for ALL of them, we are called to LOVE THEM, to [3]TRAIN THEM up in the way that is right, AND to [4]NOT EXASPERATE THEM in the process. But what does that look like? And how on earth do we accomplish this incredible feat?

Many have undertaken the task to write books on childrearing, on the best discipline methods and how to get your kid to behave.

I am NOT doing that. I am NOT concerned about making my children look or sound right. I am not concerned about having perfect little obedient robots for children. I am concerned about the development of their character and empowering them to be the absolute best version of themselves.

---

[3] Proverbs 22:6

[4] Ephesians 6:4

Every life changing action is born out of a strong push for something. The way we parent was fashioned out of a very real, purposeful desire for our children to be equipped for this world and all that it will bring their way - the good, the bad, and the ugly.

We do this foundationally by teaching them that consequences follow every choice, whether positive or negative. And MOST IMPORTANTLY, that at 5 ANY GIVEN MOMENT they are ALWAYS offered another choice.

I want them to be able to see clearly which choices lie in front of them and have the ability and soundness of mind to choose the best one. I want to raise my children to have a solid understanding of WHY they believe what they do. Not simply because I told them something. I want my kids to learn to think deeply and not take issues at face value.

If you are feeling this same way than you picked up the right book! From here on out we will be tackling this issue one step at a time.

It is VITAL that as we set out on this parenting journey we look ahead to what our goals

---

5 Lamentations 3:22-23

are for our children, because it will set us on the path towards "Parenting on Purpose".

I am going to share with you some of my goals in parenting my children. And then I encourage you to actively write out on the following pages what is currently most important for your children.

Lydia's Foundational Parenting Goals
(only a few)

1. I want my children to know they can trust me.
2. I want my children to know that I love them unconditionally.
3. I want my children to learn to make the best choice in any given circumstance.
4. I want my children to be respectful and polite to their elders and to those in authority.
5. I want my children to love and honor their siblings.
6. I want my children to be kind and considerate of their peers.
7. I want my children to love learning.
8. I want my children to take ownership of their own life and choices.

Now it is important to note that this list contains just a few of my baseline goals. There are many more child-specific "practical application" goals as well. Goals like, 'I would like my child to understand the value in doing their homework every day, so that they will do it without me having to ask them to.' That goal might only pertain to one of my children who isn't currently doing that. These "practical application" goals can, and should be, very specific in nature to address important character issues.

Remember THIS IS NOT ABOUT BEHAVIOR MODIFICATION. This is about ESTABLISHING GOOD CHARACTER, something that is much stronger and longer-lasting and belongs to the child themselves.

It is also important to note that depending on the age of your child, as time goes on these goals will adjust. As our kids learn and develop in various ways we will be able to adapt our list to new goals.

For instance, if one of my goals is to help establish the value of a strong work ethic in my teenager, it would help if that was built upon a previously established goal of teaching them to pick up their toys when they are done. The goal grows with the age.

We live in a time and place where fear is the motivator for much of our parenting choices. And despite our best intentions, that fear brings out our most controlling tendencies. When driven by fear we inadvertently limit our child from experiencing the consequences, both good and bad, of their choice. In fact, many times we take away the idea of choice all together. 6 In a world of fear-based parenting we are going to take a different approach.

The way of Love is to give a choice and to spell out the consequences of each one BEFORE the child chooses. We will examine in this book exactly what that looks like.

MY PARENTING GOALS

_____

_____

_____

_____

_____

_____

---

6 2 Timothy 1:7

CHAPTER 2
Being a Parent on Purpose

"Like I always tell my clients - begin each day as if it were on purpose" Hitch

The quote above is from one of my all-time favorite movies, "Hitch." The first time I watched it, this line struck a chord in me.

Did you know that the average human life span (75 years) amounts to ONLY 28,000 days? At my ripe age of 35, I have already BREEZED through my first 12,775!

If it were possible for a computer to give me a truthful printout of how many of those days I begrudgingly lived through (with worry, stress, depression, anxiety, fear as my daily motivators) versus how many were spent purposely and intentionally living freely, I think the numbers would be a teeny bit saddening.

THANKFULLY, I have a choice ahead of me. I can waste some time upset at myself regarding the time that I have misused. OR I can start now to live on purpose and to look forward to all that will come as a result of that. I think I will choose the second option.

So let's get started. Let's make some purposeful changes to our own responses that will in turn impact our child's character.

STOP YOUR WHINING!

Scene:
Child: "mom, mom, mom, mommy, mumma, mum, mom, mom, mommy, mom, mumma...."

You (after about 10 minutes of this going on in the background of your brain): "WHAT DO YOU WANT?!?!!?!?!"

STOP THE WHINING! No I am not talking to your child, I am talking to YOU, Dad and Mom.

This is not a judgment time. Trust me, I have been there too. I know it well. That moment when you are in the midst of something that is taking your whole attention, perhaps it is social media or video games. Maybe it is something far more important like work or household duties, or even an important telephone call. Your child comes running up to you, pulling on your shirt, totally oblivious to what you are currently engaged in, and they are just standing there saying your name OVER and OVER and OVER again.

You are so lost in thought that you are barely even aware that they are there. Until ALL OF A SUDDEN something clicks in your brain and you are now HYPER aware that for the last twenty minutes your child has been trying to get your attention. A surge of overwhelming pressure comes over you, so you do what every normal parent does and FREAK OUT at your kid.

This situation can broaden into others as well; all those times when your child is not necessarily even trying to get your attention, but they are misbehaving in various ways, fighting with their siblings, running around inside the house screaming at the top of their lungs (just for fun of course), or just being annoying.

Suddenly you break out of your reverie and snap to attention. From somewhere deep inside, you pull out your most scary authoritative of voices and yell something to the effect of "CUT IT OUT!!!"

And really what we are saying is "LEAVE ME ALONE TO DO WHAT I WANT TO DO!"

One of the greatest traps that even the best of parents can fall into, is allowing yourself to feel like your child's misbehavior is an inconvenience to you. We are going to shift our paradigm a little bit. NOW, instead of shutting them down, we are going to....

SEIZE THE MOMENT!

[7] The greatest responsibility we have ever been given is to raise our children well. That means taking those moments seriously. Not being "put off" by our children's presence but instead cultivating an understanding that your MAIN JOB during the first 18 years of their life is to help them respond to life well.

Now I can assure you this does not mean that your child should get away with bad behavior or with saying your name over and over endlessly. We will get to "addressing" those types of situations in a later chapter.

But for now we must get our own head in order. We must make the most of the time that we are given to raise these children well.

EVERY instance of negative behavior MUST BE SEEN as a moment you are given to train them in a better way! And EVERY moment of good choices, or good responses to their situation, is a moment to encourage them that it was noticed and you are proud of them. SO START SEIZING THOSE MOMENTS!

To parent well, we must parent on purpose. No more just getting through the day with my

---

[7] Proverbs 22:6

children as an aggravation or as an afterthought. When you wake up in the morning take a look at your goals. Take a quick minute to pray for each one of your kids and for you to be a good leader in helping them address their character.

I realize that there are some days when you feel just so worn out, you need a break and you just "can't handle it anymore." I will tell you that being intentional IS the key to making your hard day better.

Your child's misbehavior, if unaddressed, will continue to go on in the background of your day, regardless of if you are tired or not. And it will wear you out in ways you can't even describe. Your saving grace is to address it right away. Because once it is handled well, you will get the much needed peace that you were yearning for in the first place.

REMEMBER: YOU SET THE TONE FOR COMMUNICATION!

Your responses as the parent, set the foundation for your child's ability to communicate. If you are able to stay calm and address each situation with a clear mind, not out of unchecked emotions or frustrations, your child will quickly learn that they don't need to yell or scream to be heard either.

When we shift our paradigm from being frustrated or inconvenienced by our children, and instead, recognize our role in those moments, we shift the whole tone of the interaction.

IT IS IMPERATIVE that you do not punish your child simply because you are mad at their behavior. That will only turn around and bite you in the butt. Instead of recognizing their wrong, the child will see that they are getting punished because you are upset. It will only succeed in making your child resent you and your feelings. And in turn it will start a break down in relationship and communication.

Parents, get yourself together, calm yourself down, and take the time that you need so that you can effectively RESPOND to your child instead of REACTING to them. Your relationship with your child will GREATLY benefit from this one (not so simple) adjustment. But don't worry the more you practice responding, the EASIER it will get.

You got this!

CHAPTER 3
Teaching the "Why Factor"

Recently, one of my children was caught in the midst of a lie. It was one of those circumstances where there was absolutely no reason to lie at all. He wasn't afraid of getting in trouble, he just completely made something up and presented it as truth to the rest of the family. This child was sharing, just in normal conversation, an interaction he had supposedly had the day before.

I could immediately tell that something wasn't quite right with his story. It was either greatly exaggerated or completely made up.

This was not the first time that this had happened. In fact, I have had several conversations with this child regarding the devastation that even seemingly harmless falsehoods can cause. We have talked about the breakdown of trust and how lying will impact relationship in negative ways. We talked about who we are and how we would like people to see us. Would we like to be known as honest, or as a liar? Would we rather be seen as trustworthy or unreliable?

Because of the foundation of conversation that has been laid, when this situation took place, I immediately halted the whole conversation. I said "Wait a minute. Everyone stop talking for a second. I want us to readjust ourselves to really consider what is the truth, what really happened. If we are to be trustworthy people we can only allow truth to come out of our mouths."

It was silent for a couple minutes and then my child began to speak again. This time he readjusted his account to something that was clearly a more truthful version of the interaction that took place.

When that happened, my other children began to interject "Wait, so you are saying this part NEVER happened? Wait, so no one hit anyone else in the face?" etc. I again stopped the conversation and redirected everyone. "We are in the midst of a learning time guys. Every single one of you have been in this situation yourselves and we are going to have grace for their process. He stopped and readjusted back to the truth so we are not going to make him feel foolish right now." Each one agreed and we moved on with our day.

Because we had previously had this conversation this child knew the choices in front of them and the consequences of each. 8We need to understand that character building is a PROCESS and if we lay the foundation well, future interactions will benefit from it.

---

8 2 Peter 1:5-8

[9]If we can accept that, even for the best of us, character building can take time and practice, then we must not see our child's process as a series of failures but rather continued opportunities to solidify what was laid in the foundation.

LAYING THE FOUNDATION

I believe that the effectiveness of our parenting decisions correlate directly with the level of trustworthiness we have established in our child's eyes. Did you read that? Take a second and read it again because it is important.

Have you established a foundation of trust with your child? This comes pretty naturally (in normal parental settings) in the earliest days of your child's life outside the womb. All that your child can do is trust that you will cater to his/her every need. And we certainly do our best.

But what about as they get older? How do we establish trustworthiness?

"Practice What You Preach"

My husband and I used to be youth pastors at a local congregation. We had a large variety of

---

[9] Proverbs 24:16

kids from various backgrounds and experiences, some having grown up within the context of the church and some not at all.

Parents would come to me regarding their teen's behavior and when I would speak to the kid they seemed to have just as much to say about their parent's behavior at home. Your child is not stupid, they can very easily spot where your words and your actions don't line up. And the more your child sees the discrepancies, the less they will respect what you have to say.

If you are telling your child to be kind and treat people respectfully but then they hear you talking about your coworker/family member/fill in the blank, in a degrading gossipy manner, what does that show them? Ultimately doesn't that show that these characteristics that you are trying to instill in your child are not really valuable, if you don't put the time and effort into your own character?

To lay a foundation of trustworthiness you need to make sure that you are abiding by the same character principles that you put before your child. 10Your life MUST be the example for all that you are instilling in them. If not, your message, over

---

10 Matthew 7:12

time, will get thrown out the window, and so will any respect that your children might have had for your instruction to them.

When you SHOW your child with your actions the same thing that you are speaking to them with your words, THEN you will be effective in helping build their character.

Many people change personality when they are in the comfort of their own home. They behave one way out in public when the world is watching, but at home their interactions with their spouse or children are anything but kind or gracious. THIS MUST NOT BE.

[11] Your words and your actions must align with each other. If it is important enough for your child, it must be important enough for you.

When you show your child the value of these lessons with your own life choices, even if you are still in process with these character traits, they will be drawn to learn from you more. Your child needs to know that their parents are not double-minded.

"Because I Said So!"

This is one of those phrases that gets me every time. Although I do believe there is a time

---

11 James 1:22

and a place for this phrase, it gets so overused by parents who either don't feel like taking the time OR don't know how to explain to their children WHY something is wrong.

This cannot become our default statement to our kids. WE must learn to THINK about the "WHY" factor.

WHY is it important that my child does not talk back to me when I am asking them to do something? (Because in order for them to one day be successful at a job or in school, they need to be willing and able to take instruction)

WHY is it so important not to take someone else's things without first asking permission? (Because in the real world, that is considered stealing and you could go to jail, OR because you would not like someone to take your things without asking. That would really make you not want to be friends with that person)

WHY is it important that we are not mean to our siblings? (They are people who have feelings as well. No person should be treated meanly)

Those answers can obviously be simplified or gone more into depth depending on the age and understanding of the child. Foundationally, our children need to know that we don't just say things "because." There is ALWAYS a reason.

There are some "WHYS" that my children may not understand at a certain age and so I make sure I tell them, "I am asking that you trust me on this one, and we will get to this when you have a little more understanding of things"

THIS IS SO IMPORTANT! 12 It is only when we have established that we practice what we preach AND that there is ALWAYS a reason for what we say, that we can justify a "Because I said so." Our children will not resent that answer so much because it is not being overused.

That being said, there ARE TIMES where you will not have the opportunity to explain to your child the "why" because you need them to do something immediately. It is imperative to me that my child will obey in an instant at a young age because I know that there are dangers for which they have no grid of understanding. The classic example is telling them to not touch the hot stove or to stop them from running into the street after a ball. The obedience should come before the explanation because your child knows that you always have a reason for what you say.

This also pertains to your older child. I will give you a random example of how this could be played out in real life, because we know real life is all random situations anyways.

---

12 1 Peter 3:15

Say your teenager is out driving with her friends and you get a call from your mechanic saying that he just realized that he forgot to tighten the lug nuts on the car before you picked it up earlier. Your child isn't answering her phone so you send out text messages to her and all her friends saying "Pull over and stop driving the car immediately!" If your child knows that you always have a reason for what you say and that you are trustworthy, they are going to do what you say without an explanation, even if it seems to them like the car is driving fine. Your words will hold more weight to her than her own perception in the moment.

This level of trust and respect does not "just happen." It is cultivated and nurtured by every interaction you have with, or in front of, your child from the day they are born up until adulthood.

Make sure you lay a good foundation. Take a look at the character goals you wrote previously for your children and see if your own life matches up to them. If not, get cracking. Start bringing your own words and actions into alignment! Your parenting journey will be much smoother and effective if you do!

CHAPTER 4
Establish Choice and Consequence

As grownups, we have lived long enough to learn that in this world there are consequences, either negative or positive, dependent on every choice we make. Our children, on the other hand, are protected from much of life's realities as we play the buffer to most of their actions.

As toddlers throw temper tantrums, we, the parent are the shock absorbers for that tantrum. Because we realize the lack of understanding in our child, in reference to their actions, we do not hold them to the same standard of relationship that they will experience once they are older.

Because we are the barrier between our child and their natural relational consequences, it ALSO becomes our responsibility to put effective pseudo consequences in place that will help our child realize the danger of continuing in their bad behavior.

When our toddler fights over a toy with another child, we put our child in timeout so they can understand that if they treat other people that way, they will lose the ability to play or interact with their friends or family. It is a consequence that fits the crime in a much lesser version from the reality that would take place were the child to display that same behavior with a friend as an older teenager or an adult. In that case, they might very well lose the friendship all together.

Because we are the ones responsible for setting the consequences, both good and bad for our child, it is beneficial if we do our best to match the consequence to the choice our child has made. That means not letting every good choice be rewarded with candy and every bad choice be rewarded with timeout.

As we spoke about several chapters back, this can only be done if we remain clearheaded and do not allow ourselves to feel inconvenienced by our children. Our response to our children sets the tone for learning.

13 Punishment vs. Discipline

My husband and I have come away from the idea of punishment and opted instead for discipline in regards to our children. Many people use these two words interchangeably but for us there is a very specific difference between the two.

Miriam-Webster's Dictionary helps us understand these two terms a little bit better.

---

13 Hebrews 12:7-11

These are not the complete listing of definitions, just those that were applicable to this conversation.

Punishment:
A. Suffering, pain, or loss that serves as retribution
B. A penalty inflicted on an offender through judicial procedure
Severe, rough, or disastrous treatment

Discipline:
Training that corrects, molds, or perfects the mental faculties or moral character

When we take ownership of the fact that WE are the ones in charge of teaching and directing our children, we can no longer look at their behavior as an indicator of their own delinquencies and in need of punishment. Instead, we see the areas where our attention and focus need to be most pinpointed as we seek to discipline our child. Then we address those areas.

As it goes, a discipline and a punishment can look almost identical. What changes them is the motivator, the content of your heart. Is your response to your child born out of frustration at them and so you want to punish them, or is it born out of a desire for your children to learn and grow and be the absolute best version of themselves?

Whichever one it is, I will tell you this, your child will know the difference.

The O'Leary Order of Discipline

We have three steps that we take with our children when it comes to discipline. Maybe it will help you as you establish your parenting goals.

Step 1: Learning from Listening

When our child has shown a characteristic that is not something that we allow in our household our first step is to give them the opportunity to learn from our words.

This is where the "WHY" factor comes in. We lay the foundation. We take time to express to them the reasons why what they did was not ok. We explain to them what the real-world consequences for that look like, while engaging them in as part of the conversation. We ask them to explain back to us what we just said. We ask them to now tell us why it was not ok.

From there we ask them what they think might be a better response. We then have that conversation. Why one choice would be better than another.

When the "why" has been established we then put forth a choice for the future. When they come to this type of situation again what are their options. We spell out the consequences (the ones that we have designed for the situation) both positive and negative depending on what choice they make.

It is sometimes helpful to take a minute before addressing your child to figure out what the consequences will be. If you don't, you run the risk of giving voice to your frustration and threatening a consequence that either you cannot, or you will not, follow through on. That is not a good thing to do because it will teach your child that you don't mean what you say and it will actually SLOW DOWN the learning process.

Our hope is always that they will learn from our words. Over time, when you remain consistent in your own behavior and responses, your child will learn that the best way to learn is from Step 1, learning from listening.

Step 2: Learning from a Discipline

DC Talk put out a song in 1992 (man I am feeling really old right now) called "The Hard Way." In it the singer is expressing how "some people gotta learn the hard way." I believe this is true to an extent.

My oldest child was so incredibly easy when it came to discipline. She very rarely had to go past Step 1. I could just give her a look and she would melt and change her course. My next three children on the other hand were NOT that easy. They varied from challenging to super-challenging at times; very stubborn and very strong willed, even from infancy. But each one has come so far from the pushing stages, that they are much more apt to learn from me speaking to them than from needing anything more than that.

So, although I think many kids push for the hard way initially, I do believe that you can teach your kid while they are still young that it is better to learn the "easy way from listening."

We reach Step 2 when our child has made the choice to do again what they had been spoken to about in Step 1. This means, that while knowing the consequence that would be attached to their choice, they still decided to behave in a certain manner that is not allowed in our home.

At this juncture, we do not yell and scream, we do not berate them or tear them down, we express our sadness that now we have to follow through with the previously discussed discipline.

This is where it is very important to pick a discipline that matches the crime. You want the weight of the discipline to effect the initial desire to choose that behavior again.

For instance, if your child is constantly sneaking sugary foods and you have spoken to them about their health, how their body works, and how too much sugar can have a negative impact on how their body functions; as well as speaking to them about sneakiness and taking things that are not theirs and yet they STILL persist, it is so very important that your discipline drives the goal home.

You can completely clear out all sweets from your home for a time. On top of that they can write a paper on the negative effect that sugar has on the body. You can make them eat a head of broccoli or some other potentially unappealing yet healthy food for the next however many meals so they can realize that you value their health and they need to as well. If they won't take ownership of their own healthy eating habits than you will do it for them etc. You can figure out how long it takes to use up the energy taken in from that much sugar and make them run in place for that amount of time. Get Creative! But stay on point!

The next time they think about sneaking that piece of candy they will remember how long it took them to eat that whole broccoli crown, or how long they had to run in place and consider if it was worth it.

Fitting the discipline to the behavior is key. At the same time, when they start to change their behavior, they ask you for the candy first or they stop sneaking things, MAKE SURE YOU NOTICE IT! Be sure to say something to them! Let them know how happy you are to see them making smart, healthy choices and reward them with a treat!

Step 3: Learning from Pain

When we face the reality that persisting in bad character brings about a lot of emotional, spiritual and physical pain as we are older, it is only right that the persistence of negative choices will lead to pain in our discipline process as well.

In all honesty we have not had to get to Step 3 since our children were much younger. And the real hope and aim is that your child learns very early on that it is much better to learn from Step 1 or Step 2 than to push all the way to Step 3.

When our children were young, and there were not a lot of consequences that mattered or that they understood, our Step 3 often came in the form of a spanking. I am aware that there is great controversy regarding spanking. And I hope I have laid a very clear foundation that none of these disciplines are done with anger or frustration. If you are unable to control your anger as a parent you have no business spanking your child.

If we were ever brought to this step with our child, we were very systematic about it. We would tell our child they needed to get into the bathroom. When one of us would go in, we would make sure that we point out that we tried to teach them with our words, we tried to teach with a discipline but none of them were strong enough for them to realize the destructiveness of their behavior. We would point out that the only reason we were in that situation was because they refused to learn any other way. We cared about them too much to allow them to carry these character traits into their teen or grown up years. We would ask them to please learn from this Third Step because the pain only escalates as we persist in our bad choices.

We were not in there because we were mad at them, or because we wanted to hurt them. In fact, it was just the opposite. We did not want to be in there, and our child knew it. We were both sad at this situation.

We spanked them on their bum the same number as their age. And as they cried we picked them up on our lap and held them reiterating that it was their choice that made us both come to that place. This was not something we wanted, and this was not something they wanted, and yet, here we were because our choices have consequences.

I do not regret at all our decision to have Step 3 be a spanking. I also know there are many who do not take that route and I say "more power to you." The older our children have gotten the more they have expressed to us their gratitude that we did not let them persist in their bad choices without consequences. They see the result of lack of love and discipline in so many of their friend's lives and in their relationships with their parents. So whatever method of discipline you choose, if your heart is right and consistent in it, your child will learn from it.

Keeping your balance

The best balance for raising children is one where Love displays itself both in building up and tearing down. We build up and encourage the incredible gift of who our children are. And we tear down all that has been falsely attached to our children.

This balance is extremely important. It starts with keeping a proper perspective of who God made your child to be. When we are confident in that, then we can pour into all that your child uniquely is and we can identify and take away all that they are not.

If you are on Facebook at all you have probably seen the recent videos of parents or teachers taking the time to verbally build up their children. They speak all that is good about that child. In one video the father has the daughter repeat back to herself these things every single morning in a mirror.

I am strong.
I am smart.
I work hard.
I am beautiful.
I am respectful.
I'm not better than anyone.
Nobody's better than me.

[14]The Bible tells us that the power of life and death is in the tongue. It is such a simple thing for us to verbally affirm all that God made our child to be but yet, we have such a hard time finding the time. PARENTS, MAKE THE TIME.

But I would encourage you to go a step farther as well. Instead of just reaffirming these things directly to your child, speak to others these things ABOUT your child. Your children pick up most of your conversations with your friends. They hear how you speak about them to others. This will affirm to them that you are not just saying it

---

14 Proverbs 18:21

"because you have to say it to them" but because it is truly what you think.

When I see my child giving freely, being generous and kind, I will first make sure to mention it to them that I saw it and I thought it was wonderful. THEN I will also tell others about it in their presence. This is how we encourage growth.

The second part of this balance has to do with the influence that friends, siblings, the media, bullies, or virtually anyone else that your child might come in contact with, would say to them. This also addresses the internal voice that your child might hear that seeks to tear them down as well.

As parents, it is vitally important that we are aware of what our child is believing about themselves. There are far too many tragedies of totally unsuspecting parents losing their child to suicide. We must listen intently to our kids and take note of anything that has attached itself to them in a negative way. And then we must tear down that notion and rebuild with the truth.

We had a situation in our home where one of our daughters began to compare herself to her sister (our other daughter). And in every area of comparison she would find herself lacking. We began to take notice of this in her interactions with us, the way she would comment when our other daughter would get a compliment. We noticed that she stopped doing some of the things she used to love to do because she felt like she couldn't do it as well as her sister. She was believing a lie about her value and was beginning to adjust her behavior to reflect her belief. This was not good.

So, we began to make sure that every time we saw that lie displayed through our daughter's words or actions we caught it on the spot. We stopped her from engaging with the thought any longer, so that she would not find herself in a negative brain pattern of depression or anxiety. We addressed it, we declared it not true. We highlighted the truth. We spoke about where that thought came from. We gave her analogies to help her understand better that what she was choosing to believe was not true. And eventually she got it.

As parents, we are called not only to build up and train our child to identify the good, and the truth. We are ALSO called to train our child to identify a lie when they hear it. But that can only come by our steady involvement in the building up and tearing down balance.

Love Always Forgives

Remember we are taking the course of discipline, not punishment. Make sure that when the discipline has ended your interactions with your child are friendly and loving, not holding their choice against them. 15 For love covers a multitude of sins! Your consistent love will be your greatest tool against any voice that would tell your child that you don't really care or that they cannot confide in you.

---

15 1 Peter 4:8

CHAPTER FIVE
Teaching Personal Responsibility

In the previous chapter we talked about how, as parents, we need to maintain a balance of building up and tearing down. As our children grow they will be faced with a mean and unrelenting world. We cannot only hope that they will remember the things we have told them. We must teach them how to identify it for themselves!

Our children need to be trained to take personal responsibility for their own minds and hearts. This process begins at a fairly young age. With our children, we began around the age of 6.

With the introduction of electronic devices into childhood development and recreation, the door has been opened at a much younger age for our children to see and hear things that we would not want them to.

If your child is in public school there is a great possibility that by the age of 7, they have encountered a wide range of swear words and slang that they shouldn't even know the meaning of yet.

We can try and put as many preventative measures around what our children see, but technology is constantly changing and it seems there is no truly effective way to completely block all negative influence from our children.

To equip our children to thrive in a world full of destructive pleasures, we must teach them how their minds and bodies work. We must begin to give them freedom to make choices as to what they will watch, the type of music they will listen to, and the types of parties they will go to. But before that, we need to be confident that they have learned how to determine if something is beneficial or harmful to them.

Understanding the 5 Senses

We all know the 5 senses; sight, hearing, touch, taste, and smell. We start experiencing them all from birth. We start learning the basics of them in preschool and kindergarten. Unfortunately, that is where most of our knowledge on the subject ends.

While we continue on with our lives EXPERIENCING all of these senses and their direct impact on our brain function, our knowledge does not line up with our experience. Many people are walking around completely ignorant to the correlation between what their brain takes in through their senses and what comes out of their lives in terms of thought pattern and behavior. They say that "ignorance is bliss." Well in this case it is anything but bliss.

Our brains are like incredible super computers. The data is taken in directly through our senses. We then process that data, categorize it, and (in the simplest of terms) live it out.

During developmental years we need to teach our children how their senses connect to their behavior. For instance, if they are surrounding themselves with friends, or media that have a lot of bad language in it, the likelihood of that language coming out of their own mouths has increased exponentially. It is not an excuse for that to happen, but more a reality that the chance of it is much higher.

It is important that our children realize this connection so that we can then teach them...

Personal Responsibility.

We talked a little bit about fear-based parenting early on in this book and how we are not doing that anymore.

Fear-based parenting takes away every opportunity for your child to take personal responsibility. Fear-based parenting is putting down rules in an effort to protect your child from everything that would seek to harm them. Fear-based parenting is a method of controlling your child's reality instead of walking them through it.

We change our God-given role of "teacher" to a false idea of "protector" not realizing that the greatest protection that we can give our child is to educate them well.

Although this "protection" method might work well for the first 18 years of your child's life, it can have disastrous consequences in their future.

If a child has only ever been "protected" and not "taught," when they encounter things that they have never experienced, or issues they have never wrestled with, they will have no foundation for decision making. They will essentially be left to the mercy of whatever information comes their way from their peers or professors.

All you need to do is look up the statistics of how many children leave the faith at the age of 18 years old. It is because by that age they are encountering life situations that they are totally unprepared for. They have never learned the "Why." They have lived off of "because my parents said so."

It is embarrassing as a young adult to be faced with thought processes and situations that so many other people hold confident opinions about, when they have no idea of their own thoughts. People who are unsure or have not learned to examine an idea, tend to gravitate towards people who sound like they know what they are talking about. I mean, at least they are confident, right? And if our children have not learned to question thought processes, how on earth will they question what sounds so "put together" by their friends or teachers?

We must TEACH our kids now, personal responsibility for their own mind, and ALLOW them to wrestle with the various results.

This can be hard and scary. But if you have laid a foundation of trustworthiness, if you have shown that you practice what you preach, if you always work to show them the "why," if you have effectively put in place discipline measures that match the choices that have been made, this will come a lot easier than you can imagine. Your child will already be much more self-aware than most of their peers at this point in life and will be ready and feeling privileged for this type of responsibility given.

So, what does this look like?

It is important to start with small, easily monitored situations to allow our children to build "trustworthiness" and "good character." And to allow situations where they can also begin to learn a little bit better how their eyes and ears process things.

We allow our children the "freedom" (obviously within reason) to choose what shows or movies they would like to watch. Maybe they have heard from a friend about an awesome show and they want to check it out too.

I remember one time when our kids were much younger they wanted to watch a Scooby Doo Movie. I knew it would possibly be a little scary for them but I allowed them to make the decision to watch it. Lo and behold, later that night two of my girls couldn't sleep because of having watched that movie, so that became a teaching time.

My girls now had a personal experience to back up what we were teaching them. They were now realizing how difficult it can be when something gets in your brain and you can't seem to stop thinking about it. Over the course of the next couple days the cartoon images would come back to their minds periodically and we would talk about it.

That experience became foundational for those girls in choosing what they wanted to watch. They began to understand themselves a little better and the value of protecting their eyes and ears.

I love superhero movies and allow my kids to watch some of the "lesser" graphic ones. But even in those I see there are times when my girls will purposely cover their eyes because they don't want to see an image that might get stuck in their brains. They are protecting their thought processes. They are learning wisdom and they are learning their limitations.

I just want to clarify in case anyone reading this is thinking "wow they let their children choose anything they want to watch." NO! We put parameters around what is "allowable" in our home. But we would rather our children learn in a safe and accountable place, and at a young age, how media impacts our minds.

I do not want my child having their first experience of this self-realization while being a teenager watching something entirely inappropriate at a friend's house, feeling stuck on their own, not knowing how to handle the ramifications, and feeling like they are going to get "punished" if they tell us.

I want my child prepared WAY before that time. I want them already aware that they have no desire to watch something inappropriate or destructive because they absolutely do not want it stuck in their mind and stealing from their day.

Now if there is a time where one of my children has chosen to watch something, or listen to something that they know would be damaging to their mind or heart. When we find out about it, we, then, go into our Three Steps of Discipline plan in hopes to help them establish a lasting change in their character.

So when do we start these conversations?

In the younger years the focus should mostly be on the Eye and Ear senses. And if you are feeling like you are unsure of when to start these conversations, have no fear! It will become evident when the time has come.

The first of many future conversations came for me years ago. My oldest daughter was roughly six years old. It was a beautiful day. We were all at the beach. The sun was shining. The kids were playing. Things were looking good.

My oldest daughter was building a sandcastle. She had spent a significant amount of time on it. She is very much an artist and truly cares about how her work comes out. So, when her younger siblings went racing across her beautiful castle, she was VERY upset.

I watched her from a little distance to see what would happen next. Well, after a little bit she came over to me with her head hanging low.

"Brooklyn, what's the matter hunny?" I asked her.

"The kids ran over my sandcastle and I had worked so hard on it!" She was clearly upset.

"Man that stinks Brookie."

"Yeah, but mom I need to tell you something."

"What's that?"

"I was so angry at the kids when they did that, that I swore."

"You swore?" I was a little surprised that my 6 year old would even know any swears at that point.

"Yeah, in my head."

"Oh so you THOUGHT a swear. What swear did you think Brookie?"

"Ass" She sheepishly replied.

Now I will tell you it took every bit of strength inside of me to not let out the laughter that was forming in HUGE waves in my belly. The picture of my little girl mentally saying "ass" while her siblings were running through her sandcastle was almost enough to make me lose all composure. But thankfully I held it together.

"Hmmm, Where did you hear that word Brooklyn?"

"In Harry and the Hendersons" Ah, a movie we had watched together as a family.

"How did it make you feel to think that word?"

"I didn't like it"

"Yeah, those type of words don't feel really good. Do you know how that word got to be in your brain?"

"From the movie?"

"Yup, this is one of those reasons why we need to make really careful choices about what we let into our ears and eyes. Did you know that you can change your mind so that you won't think that word again?"

"I can?"

"Yup, why don't you go back over to where your sandcastle was and think about what just happened, but THIS time pick a DIFFERENT word, one that feels better and maybe kinder in your mind. Because you have a choice for what your brain thinks."

So Brookie skipped back over to her sandcastle and thought for a bit and changed a pattern that was starting to form in her mind. When we were all done, she came back to me and we talked about what she chose to think instead. The second time around was MUCH better and kinder.

The point of this story is to show you that, if you are paying attention, you will see when your child is ready to start this conversation. You just need to seize the moment to teach them some understanding about how we are all made.

Each of my children have had their own personal stories of starting down this path of taking responsibility for their thoughts and actions.

As they grow, the conversations reach to more topics and greater "whys." The kids engage and are welcome to ask whatever questions they want. And when they ask questions I will never make fun of their thought processes.

Into the teenage years the topics of taste, touch and smell enter in more. With the rapid escalation of drugs and sex into adolescent culture, we cannot shy away from training our kids about the effect that these things have on their brains and who they are.

Trust your instinct for when these conversations are appropriate. If you feel ill-equipped or don't know if you have answers to some of these questions, take some time and do a little research. You can even have your child do research with you and compare what you find. Do not be afraid of conversation. Above all else be INTENTIONAL!

CHAPTER SIX
Honestly Speaking

^{18}Fix these words of mine in your hearts and minds; tie them as symbols on your hands and bind them on your foreheads. ^{19}Teach them to your children, talking about them when you sit at home and when you walk along the road, when you lie down and when you get up. ^{20}Write them on the doorframes of your houses and on your gates, ^{21}so that your days and the days of your children may be many in the land the LORD swore to give your ancestors, as many as the days that the heavens are above the earth." Deut 11

Sometimes it feels like everything in this world is designed to keep us from truly, authentically, communicating. It is amazing really, so many mediums of communication and what we have gotten from those is a breakdown in REAL relationship.

Social media seems to promote people talking "at" each other, not "to" them. I see so many people vaguely venting about situations to a massive audience instead of going individually, in person, to someone to work out the given situation.

Text and instant messaging, on the other hand, while they involve two people having a conversation, they are completely devoid of facial expression and verbal intonation, so the words take on whatever tone the reader assumes the writer is giving forth. More often than not, the reader is mistaken and feelings are needlessly hurt.

We also see that through non-verbal communication, pictures and videos posted up on Facebook, Instagram, Snapchat, and Twitter, people are trying to portray relationships, lifestyles, family time, and even their own features in such an overtly fantastic way as to "boast" on something that is just a surface reality. Instead of drawing people deeper in, it often alienates those who then look at their own lives through not-so-rose-colored-glasses and begin to feel envious of those who appear to "have it all together". While the appearance on these sites is that we have "lots of friends" or followers, the reality is very few are people who we truly have authentic friendships with.

We must face the fact that we, as parents, carry the massive responsibility of teaching our kids to communicate well. And one of the foundations of good communication is

SELF-CONFIDENCE!

"Confidence in oneself and in one's powers and abilities"
Miriam-Webster Dictionary

Now, self-confidence is an interesting thing. It is confidence in something that is within one's self or ability. I think this confidence is often misunderstood. So let me clarify exactly what I am getting at.

The typical picture of self-confidence involves someone who is so "confident" in their "superior abilities", that they have no problem speaking about them and not being swayed by anyone else's opinion or thought.

That is NOT the self-confidence I am seeking to portray. The confidence that I promote in my kids is a realization that they have nothing to prove. Their value does not come from how much they know or if they are always right. In the same way, if they don't know something or are wrong about something that doesn't impact their value either.

This self-confidence come from an understanding that learning is a beautiful thing. That NO ONE has it all completely figured out and therefore every conversation is an opportunity to learn and to grow. It is a place of giving and receiving of ideas. It is a stance born out of humility and desire for understanding, not pride.

So self-confidence in conversation is realizing that a conversation does not define anyone. It is a tool to grow, whether in knowledge,

or in relationship, or in practice. And guess where your children learn this,
FROM YOU!

No Agenda Conversations

Have you ever just asked your child their opinion on something? Have you ever just listened and learned the way that they think? A common mistake parents make is to always feel like a conversation needs to come to a final conclusion where your child agrees with you. Often it is the parent telling the child something rather than walking them through the process of thinking critically.

We have a young 13 year old girl currently living at our house. On our drives to and from school and various events I ask her about her day. This is a little bit of how our conversations would go at the beginning.

"Hey! So how was school today?"
"It was alright."
"What was 'alright' about it?"
"I don't know"
"Well, let's think for a minute. What did you do today?"
"I don't know, school work."
"Ok so what type of school work did you do? What classes did you have?"

"Well I had math and history."
"Did you learn anything new?"
"Yeah we learned about the Great Depression"

This conversation went on for several minutes before I ever found out how her day really went. This was not because she was trying to hide information from me, or because she didn't want to talk about it. It was simply because she was not practiced at thinking deeply about anything. Even still, it is difficult for her to identify why she may have "liked" something or why something was "boring."

My point in sharing this interaction is to show you the vital role you play in teaching your kids how to think and to self-assess. Our children need to be taught to think a little deeper. If they like something, then WHY do they like it? If something was difficult, WHAT made it difficult?

Practice having these "no-agenda" conversations with your kids. This is your way of helping them learn to go deeper with their thoughts and engage with their own feelings on things. This will ALSO help you lay a foundation for

Tackling the Tough Topics

We have all seen those humorous confrontations in the movies of the awkward parent trying to talk to their confused kids about "the birds and the bees." It kind of puts a sinking feeling in your stomach, doesn't it?

HAVE NO FEAR! Conversations with your child DO NOT need to look or feel like that. If you have begun to lay a foundation of teaching your child to think deeper and process their own feelings and perspectives, you will not find yourself playing the role of the awkward parent. Your child will already be at the place where you converse with them regularly. They will have spoken with you and processed through their feelings and thoughts on everyday types of issues and circumstances.

Because of the depth of relationship this cultivates, you will not be "that parent" pulling out a conversation from thin air to a child who has never spoken with you about anything serious.

And because your life reflects something to your child they will want to listen and to believe what you have to say. This is both wonderful and dangerous.

As I am sure you are all very well aware, we just had an incredibly intense national election process between two candidates who were polar opposites. (Donald Trump and Hillary Clinton) Their supporters were also all vehemently opposed to anyone who thought any differently from themselves. During that time I noticed something interesting happen in my home. My children began to take a very strong stance that modeled mine and Jim's. They would speak confidently about lowering the debt or defunding Planned Parenthood. But I knew they had no idea what they were really talking about.

Every debate we watched as a family, my children would ask, "Was that good what he said Mom?" or "Was that something bad?" and I realized the power I held in that moment. With one word I could tell my kids yes or no and they would take it at face value.

This is an incredible thing to be able to say. And it is something that my husband and I have worked towards. Our children trust us. They trust the way we think. They trust the way we process situations and they know we always have a reason "why" for what we believe. We hope to maintain that trustworthiness in their eyes.

The dangerous thing about this situation is that it could be very easy for us to instill a very strong belief about something, in an impressionable child without teaching them how we got to that thought and without presenting to them all of the reasons why others might think differently as well.

I have seen people who, as teenagers, held a very strong belief on something, probably handed down by their parent's very strong belief. But because they had never encountered the "other side" of the issue, they were totally unaware of what to do with it when they were confronted as a young adult; especially when the "other side" really seemed to make more sense to them. There are also those who hold so strongly to their parent's belief or perspective that they, unwitting, join into dangerous mindset and stay stuck in it regardless of outside conversation, like in the instances of racial prejudice or the KKK. As a parent, we need to be very careful about the power and sway that we have over our children's young minds.

For instance, my husband and I are passionately pro-life. We are praying for the ending of abortion. We have taken in young pregnant, homeless, addicted women and helped be the solution so that their child's life would be saved. Our words and our life match up. Our kids have seen the fruit of our choices and have taken on this pro-life stance for themselves. THAT IS WONDERFUL and it is something I am thrilled about.

The EASY thing for me to do would be to ONLY talk to them about how "right" we are and how "wrong" anyone else would be in this situation. But I am well aware that things are never so cut and dry in real life and conversations. I am well aware that these issues of life and abortion go so much deeper and farther than the typical 'talking points' allow. And more than anything else I want my children to grow to walk in

Understanding and Compassion

Not just concepts or ideas. We want our children to value life, all life. So that means learning to understand the viewpoints of people around you and having compassion in that place. Our media wants us to believe that anyone who thinks differently is an idiot or uneducated. I do not want my children to ever demean or put another person down in that way. I want them to walk in understanding and to be self-confident and to learn to wrestle with all the difficult messy situations that life puts before them.

So when I begin to see that my child is taking a stance that mirrors mine or my husband's, I begin to question them on it. I pull them into hypothetical situations and ask their thoughts about them. I call them to wrestle with the very things that I have had to wrestle with and when they are confused and frustrated because things are never as "easy" as we would like to make them seem. I share with them my journey and how I came to believe the way that I do.

Our children cannot live on our experiences. They must be allowed their own. It is so incredibly important that we establish good, loving, healthy relationships with our kids so that we can model for them a life well lived.

As parents we are the "safe place" for our kids. If we can allow them the space to wrestle with these ideas while they are still in our home, they will come out the other side ready for whatever may lay ahead of them.

As they venture into college or the workforce, they will be standing on a very steady foundation that THEY helped build, not something that was just told to them over and over again.

CHAPTER SEVEN
Pointing Your Child to Jesus

The absolute BEST thing my parents ever did for me was introduce me to Jesus. I was raised in a Christian home from birth, but Jesus got a hold of my heart when I was around 6. It was amazing. He was truly my best friend. I would sit with Him and we would talk all the time about everything.

My parents taught me, but Jesus filled me. When I was upset, I would sit with Jesus. When I had a difficult day, Jesus would talk with me. I LOVED going to church every Sunday because I could just FEEL God with me and all around me during that time.

As parents, we need to realize that Jesus is the only One who can make a person whole. So, as much as we want to be the answer to all of our children's problems, our children need someone so much bigger and steadier than we could ever be.

I cannot express to you the joy and relief that washed over me as each of my children had their own encounter with Jesus. Because from there, a weight was lifted off of my shoulders.

I remember as a child, times of getting in trouble (rightly so) and being so mad at my parents. In those moments their words didn't seem to have an impact because I was so upset. I would then sit with God on my bed and He would calm me down. He would bring me back to peace in a way that no person could ever do. And He would show me the areas in my own heart that needed addressing.

Those experiences with the Lord have had an impact on how I relate to my own children.

Several weeks ago, one of my daughters, Autumn, was having a difficult day. We were getting ready to bring her to the mall to get her ears pierced with her cousin. A couple of the other kids in the house wanted to come as well. Autumn was in a little bit of a mood and was demanding that no one else comes. She was trying to take control of the situation and dictate how everything would go. I know that my daughter, Autumn, has a deep relationship with Jesus and the conversation I was having with her was not going anywhere productive. So I stopped the conversation and said

"Autumn, go take a walk with Jesus."

"But Mom, I don't want anyone else to come with us to the mall!"

"Autumn, GO TAKE A WALK WITH JESUS."

It didn't seem like an appropriate time to set a discipline because I could see that it was more something that she was wrestling with in her heart and mind. I knew she just needed some time with her best friend to settle her down. So she stormed off, grabbing her jacket and boots, and took her walk.

When she came back her whole face was different. She had a completely different attitude. And she was ready to go to the mall with everyone.

I have come to recognize my place as the parent to my child. They are not fully mine. They belong to God first, and then they are entrusted to me to love well, to train up in godliness and to continually point them to Him. It is my place to model and display the love of God through me so they see how good He truly is. And I take this role very seriously. But as much as I can talk with my kids, ONLY JESUS can make them whole.

Praying with your children

Because we are called to point our children to Jesus, we set aside time every day to sit with God. Most mornings a week, before we do anything else, we have quiet time. Everyone comes out to the couch. We have worship music playing, and the kids read their Bibles or just sit quietly talking to the Lord. We then go into a time of praying for people who are on our prayer board. As a parent, I am helping teach my kids how to set aside time for specific interaction with God and praying for others.

    Ever since our children were born we would pray with them before bed time. As they began to learn how to speak, we would pray for them and then we would ask them to pray for us. We didn't realize at the time what a powerful thing this would turn out to be. To this day my children are so quick to pray for Jim and myself, not just at bedtime. If they ever see us hurt or upset, they pray for us. If we have a big situation on our hands, they pray for us. And every night at bedtime, they pray for us. It has helped our children realize that we need Jesus just as much as they do, maybe even more. And they have seen their prayers answered as God moves through our lives, when they pray.

    Several years back we began to implement prayer during dinner time. Now that might sound very normal but it has a little twist to it. At our dinner time EVERYONE takes a turn to pray. We ask who would like to say "thank you" to Jesus first and immediately every hand shoots up in the air. We pick someone to start us off. Once that person has prayed they get to pick who prays next. Because our house is always full at dinner time, ranging anywhere from 10-20 people this can take quite a long time. SO we do not wait until everyone is done to eat (the food would be stone cold.) We give thanks the entirety of the meal.

I am convinced that the more we give our children opportunity to pray, the deeper their relationship with Jesus will go. I remember one morning waking up with an excruciating pain in my neck and back. The pain traveled all the way down my arm any time I attempted to turn my head. I was sitting on my bed wondering how in the world I was going to get through that day when my daughter Jedayah came in. At the time she was probably 6 or 7 years old. She crawled up on my bed next to me and asked what was wrong.

I believe a normal tendency as a parent can be to push your child away when you are in pain. The last thing you want at that moment is someone pulling on you for something. I have learned that it is incredibly important to allow your children in to those moments.

So when Jeda asked what was wrong I told her.

"My back is REALLY hurting me this morning. I can't even turn my head a little bit."

I could see the concern immediately on her face.

"Jedayah, would you please pray for me, for this pain to go away?"

Without hesitation Jedayah put her hand on my back and prayed for me. It was a very simple, childlike prayer. But the moment she was done I literally had no more pain in my back and neck. I couldn't believe it.

"JEDAYAH! Jesus just healed my back!"

She smiled at me with a HUGE smile. I said, *"Let's take a minute to thank Him!"*

So we did.

That moment encouraged both myself and Jedayah in our journeys with Jesus. Since that time, we have had our kids pray with us during many difficult situations. Times when we had no money for food or for bills, I would gather the kids together and we would pray. Times when friends or family were sick or going through difficult times we would pray. And what happened was that our children began to see God answer them. They would see miraculous provision the day we prayed. Or we would hear testimonies from our friends and family of what God had done. And it encouraged all of us.

If we remained in our fear based parenting, where we try to protect our children from our struggles, they might have missed out on the struggle, but they would have ALSO missed out on the miracles. NOW, instead of just Jim and myself having miraculous stories to tell, our children do too, because it is their story as well!

Parents, take time to encourage your children in the Lord. Pray for them, pray with them, and have them pray for you. For they will be an encouragement and a strength to you as you grow older.

Listening with your children

Just as important as praying, we must teach our children to listen. God DESIRES to speak to and through your children. It is not enough to just tell your child that God wants to speak to them. WALK THEM THROUGH THE PROCESS!

I remember one night sitting with my youngest child Ronan. He was 5 years old and he had expressed to me that God didn't talk to him, that he could never hear God.

I started out by explaining to him that God speaks to people in MANY different ways. He can speak audibly, He can speak to our spirit, He can speak through pictures, through dreams or visions, through another person to you, through memories or really any way that He wanted. We just needed to get to know God better, so we would recognize that He was speaking. I explained to Ronan that God would teach him how to hear and understand better.

I took him to the beginning of the book of Jeremiah where God begins to teach Jeremiah how to see and understand the pictures that God would give him. Ronan thought that was so amazing!

I asked Ronan if he thought that maybe God would want to speak to him in the same way. Let's try it! I took out a piece of paper and a pencil.

"Ok, close your eyes Ronan. Let's wait quiet a minute and see if a picture comes to your mind."

20 seconds went by.

"Ok! I have a picture Mom!"

Me, trying not to be skeptical of how fast that was, *"What did you see?"*

"I saw a picture of a baseball player getting ready to hit the ball."

"OK. Let's close our eyes again and see if you get anything else."

I blinked for half a second.

"I got another picture Mom!"

"Ronan, are you sure? Let's wait a minute and let God talk"

"OK, but I already know what He showed me"

"*What is it?"*

"It was a minion getting ready for a hug"

"Uh huh…"

This went on two more times where God gave Ronan a picture. Each picture was completely different and unique. And even though I found myself wondering if this was really God or my child's vivid imagination I was determined to follow the course in showing my son that God DID want to speak to Him.

When I had written each of the pictures down, I said to Ronan, "Now, we are going to ask God what the pictures mean, so we can have some understanding of what HE wants to say to you."

We closed our eyes again. *"Mom, I think I know what God is saying to me."*

"Really! That is great! What do you think He is saying?"

"In each of my pictures someone is waiting for something good to happen. So I think God is telling me that something exciting is going to happen today. I think I am going to go to a sleepover at Elijah's house and I need to get ready."

At this point I just wanted to shake my head and laugh. Nicely played Ronan, nicely played. He managed to work this "listening" time into a solid need for a sleepover at his cousin's house.

"Well," I said. *"The pictures do all have someone waiting for something exciting, so we will watch and see if something happens. And if you feel like you want to get ready for a sleepover go for it, but I am not sure if that is what it really is."*

Well Ronan did get ready for a sleepover. And about an hour later my brother called. He and his son Elijah were going to have a "Boys night" at the house because his wife and daughter were both gone for the evening. So they were wondering if Ronan could come sleep over.

Now mind you, that had not happened in months. I put down the phone completely in shock and told Ronan.

"I know Mom. I am already packed. God told me to get ready."

That experience taught us both a lesson. For me I saw that God is not limited in only speaking about deep profound things. What I had said to my son was actually true. God will speak in any way that He wants to AND about anything that He wants to.

For Ronan, he saw that God DID want to speak to him. And that God wanted to tell him EXCITING things. That has spurred him on to WANT to listen to God.

So parents, as you teach, be open to learning as well. Don't put God in a box as you are teaching your children to expect great things!

Reading the Word with your children

As you teach your child to listen, it is imperative that you are teaching them to read the Bible. Read it to them before they are old enough to do it on their own. Tell them Bible stories. Show them the nature and character of God in the historical accounts of the Israelites and the life of Jesus.

God desires to speak to your children, but there are a million other voices that are vying for your child's attention as well. Your child needs to learn who God is, so they can sift through the muck and recognize the Truth.

The more your child comes to know the characteristics of God and what His word says for their lives, the less chance there is that they will be deceived by a false reality of who they are and what this world is really about.

Ministering with your children

Because we are charged with training our children up in godliness, it is very important that we also include our children in as many church or ministry opportunities that we are involved in. Whether we are helping the poor, handing out clothing, leading worship somewhere, our children should be right beside us doing the same thing. They are seeing and participating in the love of God displayed in action.

Our children have been right beside us as we have loved the poor and the broken, the prostitute and the drug addict. We are the ones who show them that "perfect Love casts out fear". We show them discernment. Our children are interning on our lives. We are to pass on to them all that we know, and so much of what we know is experiential.

If you do not currently do ministry as a family, then start to get creative! Bake some brownies for a new neighbor. Mow the yard of the single mom in your neighborhood. Visit the local nursing home and spend time with the senior citizens. See what opportunities are available through your church gathering and sign yourselves up! There are so many ways we can extend ourselves, you just need to get intentional.

Being the church with your children

Jim and I pastor a church that meets in our home. So our dynamic and experience with this is different than most traditional settings. But I believe it can be translated in to most other experiences.

As each of our children gave their lives to the Lord, we would have them participate in our church gatherings, whether it was a worship service, prayer meeting or anything else. Have you ever heard the expression "There is no Junior Holy Spirit"? Basically, it is saying that the same big God in our lives is actively leading our children as well. And if that is truly the case, then they are a vital part of the church and should learn to participate in the church meetings.

²⁶ What then shall we say, brothers and sisters? When you come together, each of you has a hymn, or a word of instruction, a revelation, a tongue or an interpretation. Everything must be done so that the church may be built up.

As our children sit in our meetings, we provide them with paper and crayons. We encourage them to sit quietly to listen to God to see if He has something for them to contribute to the meeting. More often than not, the children bring forth some of the most profound contributions. As they are young it tends to be simple drawings, or a song that God gives them. As they grow older and can read and write, it branches out into passages of scripture or even whole Bible stories. As everyone is sharing what God is saying, the kids see how the picture they got fits right into the overall message of what God has to say to everyone. There is certainly a learning curve to all of this. There are times when I have had to question my child whether they were just coloring or if they truly felt like God gave them a picture. But the overall point is to allow for your child to participate in the gathering. And then you train them as they go.

We have often had children open up our meeting with prayer. There are lots of ways that our children can be engaged.

I do know that it can sometimes be difficult for adults to focus when children are present in the room. We teach the grown-ups to be responsible with their own attention span. They should be able to focus on the Lord even if there are distractions around. These are conversations worth having with your pastor if you feel like this would not be currently welcome in your meeting.

Children are a vital part of the church. It is important that you recognize this and teach your child this as well. I am telling you, they will exceed your expectations!

Parents, the most valuable thing you could ever do is introduce your child to Jesus. So do it! In your words, in your action, through your love and compassion, show your kids who Jesus is. Talk about Him all the time in everyday life. Bring your children into the reality of the faith. Because once they have an encounter with Jesus, their lives will never be the same!

CHAPTER EIGHT
Letting Them Grow and Letting Them Go

We have a young boy named Michael that has lived with us since he was born. He is currently three and a half years old, and boy is he a handful. I have never seen a child filled with quite so much energy and imagination as this little one is. From the moment he opens his eyes in the morning to the moment he closes them for bed, he is roaring around, his imagination giving life to every object he sees.

That being said, he is a lovable little guy with so much to offer this world. Just sometimes his energy seems to get in the way. He is bigger than his peers and super strong so he can get carried away. Whether he is hugging me goodnight or giving a friend a "tag" on the back, his well-meaning affection and overall goofiness can become painful very quickly for those around him.

His mother and I have been recently having conversations about their interactions. Michael has an excuse and a reason for everything. He has an argument for just about anything you would say to him. His mom is an incredible lady who has given her everything towards building a good life and future for her and her little man, but sometimes she can get completely worn out by his persistence and determination.

One of the conversations we have had recently is, 'What is appropriate for a three-year-old?' in terms of discussion of discipline. At that age, there is no reason that Michael is going to give that will justify any of his bad behavior. And it becomes detrimental when you find yourself in this trap of unending explanations for what you are doing and why. Michael is content to argue with you all day long about it.

This is where the beginning of the power of choice comes in. We must realize that discussion is a powerful tool that we teach our children to use wisely as they grow. At the young age of three, the teaching of communication must be at a far more foundational level than discussion and debate. We are working more on having good responses and getting help instead of getting upset.

To do this we begin to highlight the choices in front of him. Instead of a debate, the conversation goes towards, "Michael. You are not supposed to be jumping on the couch right now. I want you to be a good listener and come down. If you do not, then you will sit in the time out chair."

If Michael begins to argue about that, instead of just obeying, he is immediately moved to his consequence. In the time out chair he is told, "You did not obey, so now you have to sit here.

You can either sit here without fussing and get up in three minutes, OR if you continue to fuss and argue you can have a spank on the bum." It has taken a little bit but he is beginning to realize that he would much rather just take a time out than get a spanking.

He is getting better, as well, at coming when he is called, stopping when he is told to, and apologizing when he is asked. This is all a process that we work with to develop a foundation of choice and consequence. And it is one that is effective only when administered consistently and with just as much love as there is discipline in our interactions with him.

That being said, I have a teenager in my home as well. She is a beautiful, smart, intelligent girl who may not always see eye to eye with me or my husband.

When something comes up that she does not agree with, I absolutely do not put her in the time out chair and give the consequence of a spanking. That would be both weird and awkward for all parties involved.

The other day she wanted to go to a "tea party" (I know it sounded weird to me too) at a friend's house. From there she wanted to go to a Bible Study at another friend's house. And then from there she wanted to go to a prayer meeting down the road. That would mean an awful lot of driving for either myself or my husband. And personally, I didn't really want to do it. I had a lot to get done that day as well and I figured she didn't need to do all three things. She could focus on one, MAYBE two of them. I felt like I had a fairly reasonable argument for saying "no."

Brooklyn on the other hand, had some different thoughts about it. Number one, she had committed to bringing food to one of the events, which I do admit that I had forgotten about. Two, if she didn't go to the tea party it would be cancelled for everyone involved because there weren't enough people to justify it continuing on. That sort of thing doesn't typically phase me, but…duly noted. And thirdly, she could arrange for some of the rides between places and home so we would only have to do minimal driving in regards to her plans for the day. BINGO. That is what I needed to hear. I had no problem with it at that point.

The point is, as your child grows and changes, your interactions will grow and change as well. It is so important that you are aware and allow for that growth and change to happen. We are to be preparing our children to be productive, kindhearted, hardworking, intelligent adults. ***BUT,***

It's not all about them.

During the teenage years our children are not the only ones who need to grow and adapt. We need to be preparing ourselves for the day that they will move out. If we are not prepared, the transition during teenage years can be far more tumultuous than they need to be.

I can't tell you the number of my friends that continued doing their child's laundry, cooking all of their meals, or cleaning their rooms for them all the way up through college and beyond. It was their effort to keep their child, a child, dependent on them. But their best laid plans didn't work for them. No matter how much you might not want those childhood years to pass into adult years, IT WILL HAPPEN. So you can go through them kicking and screaming, demanding obedience without question, or you can get your heart and mind prepared for what is next to come.

I believe much of the difficulty stems from the feeling that when our child grows up we will no longer be needed. And that is a difficult thought to swallow.

But parents, that feeling is NOT TRUE. Just like your role changes from when your child is three to when they are a teen, your role changes as they become an adult. Your value and importance in their life does not and will never change. Your interactions on the other hand, should.

There is no "perfect process"

Wouldn't it be nice if we could have some sort of manual that would just give us the step by step in how to raise our children; a book that would tell us every circumstance and emotion we will face as our children grow? Unfortunately, that is an impossibility, because every child is so very unique and intricate. So we need to stop trying to find a method that will work from 0-20 and instead remember that our children aren't the only ones growing. We are too! We need to allow ourselves to grow WITH our children.

The moment you think that you have it all worked out and figured out, your child is going to change on you, or you will have another child who is completely different. (That happened to me on four separate occasions.) Either way, you are forced to interact and relate with your child and pray for heavenly wisdom to be able to adapt and be the best parent that you can be for them.

So many people have incredible difficulty navigating the teenage years. I used to work in a customer service position and therefore had regular conversation with a large variety of people. I cannot even begin to tell you the number of people who "warned me" about the teenage years. That all of a sudden my sweet innocent child will turn into a raging, rebellious, hormonal thing that I don't even recognize. Thanks for the good news folks!

I realize that I can't claim experiential knowledge on this one, as my kids are just starting into those years. But my first one is currently going through it and I have absolutely no fear whatsoever that she is going to become a monster on me.

Because every day, with every interaction, I am learning who she is little better, and she is learning who I am, and we are both learning more about ourselves. There will not be a day that she wakes up a completely different person than she was the day before. Any more than there will be a day that I wake up as someone else. I might be so preoccupied with my own life that it feels that way. But if I am intentional with each day, with my responses and interactions, we will get through this just fine.

So here we are, in the very last paragraph of the very last chapter of this book. I hope it has brought some insight and perspective on this thing we call parenting. As you embark on the greatest "calling" you have ever been given, I bless you to love your children well, and to raise them to be men and women who have learned how to choose well, as they have seen the example set before them.

Dad and Mom, you got this!